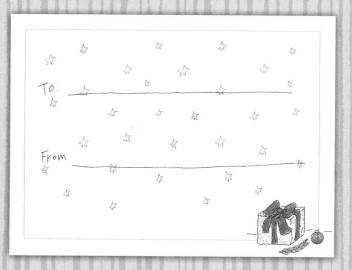

To: _____

From _____

Christmas Is a Gift

CHRIS SHEA

Published by J. Countryman, a division of Thomas Nelson, Inc, Nashville, Tennessee 37214.

Project manager—Terri Gibbs.

Designed by UDG|DesignWorks, Sisters, Oregon.

ISBN 1-4041-0182-9

http://www.thomasnelson.com
http://www.jcountryman.com

Printed and bound in the United States of America

To Mikey Shea

Everyone should be so blessed
to have a son like you.

Christmas is a gift,

a wonderful mirror

in which each of us is
still a child.

Where looking again through children's eyes brings back with sparkling clarity...

things our hearts
have cherished

and never
    quite
       outgrown.

Christmas songs we
knew by heart
and thought we had
forgotten

come floating back
in harmony
for us to sing again,

and cookies
shaped like
trees and stars

are better than
the greatest
feast.

It's always Christmas
in the heart;

Such memories
we keep
there!

The smell of a
homemade
apple pie

cooling on the
Kitchen
table,

or the feel
of a
Christmas sweater

made of
the softest wool,

even the sound a
reindeer makes tiptoeing
across a snowy roof

still lingers
in the
heart.

Love

Is the
magic ingredient
of Christmas.

It fills up
   all
 our packages,

turns an
ordinary sock

into a
Christmas
stocking

and small pines

34 ☆

into Christmas
trees.

Not even a
    city skyline

is immune
to its
magical touch.

☆37

Christmas is
a holiday

only
Love
could make,

where
mistletoe

invites
a kiss

and thoughtful gifts
of comfort
and warmth,
like slippers and robes
and
new pajamas,

remind us
that we're
loved.

Arms

hold
on
tighter,

hearts

open
wider,

and " families "

just seem
to
multiply,

because
Christmas
means
little

with
no one to
share it.

☆ 51

Christmas is not
just a date

we put
a red circle
around.

☆53

Christmas is located
deep in the heart

in a place that's
been put
there to stay....

This Christmas

may your joy be
filled to overflowing
in the company of those
you hold dear.

☆ 57

And may all
   your Christmas dreams

come true,

especially
   your dreams

of
peace
on
earth.

Merry Christmas!

Edith Kunhardt

DANNY'S MYSTERY VALENTINE

Greenwillow Books, New York

E
Kun

Library of Congress Cataloging-in-Publication Data
Kunhardt, Edith.
Danny's mystery valentine.
Summary: Danny and his mother go
in search of the person who
left Danny an unsigned valentine.
[1. Valentine's Day—Fiction]
I. Title.   PZ7.K94905Daq   1987
[E]   86-19400
ISBN 0-688-06853-7
ISBN 0-688-06854-5 (lib. bdg.)

The four-color preseparated art was printed
in yellow, red, blue, and black.
The typeface is Avant Garde Gothic Book.

Printed in Hong Kong by South China Printing Co.

For Bill, with love

One morning Danny wakes up.
He sees a letter on the floor.

He opens the letter.

Inside is a big red heart with his name on it.

"A valentine!" cries Danny.
He runs to tell his mother.

"Oh, Danny! You're lucky!" says his mother.
"But who sent it? There is no writing to say
who it's from."

Danny doesn't know. It is a mystery.
"Let's ask everybody. Please?" Danny begs.
"All right, Danny. We'll try to solve the mystery,"
says his mother.

Danny and his mother get dressed.
They go out to find out who sent the valentine.

They see Danny's friends.
"Lucy! Mark! Joshua!" Danny calls.
"Did you send me this heart?"

"No, Danny, we didn't," says Lucy. "Come on
and help us make our valentine."
"No, thank you. I have to solve the mystery,"
says Danny. "See you later."

Next Danny and his mother
visit Mr. Jones, the baker.
"Did you send me this heart,
Mr. Jones?" asks Danny.

"No, Danny, I didn't," says Mr. Jones.
"But come on back here
   and help me make some valentines."
"No, thank you, Mr. Jones. I have to
   solve the mystery. See you later."

Danny and his mother go to the stationery store. There is their friend Miss White.
"Did you send me this heart, Miss White?" asks Danny.

"No, I didn't, Danny," says Miss White.

"Please help me make this valentine."

"No, thank you," says Danny. "I have
to solve the mystery."

Danny and his mother go to the pizza store.
There is Mr. Mozzarella.
"Did you send me this heart, Mr. Mozzarella?"
asks Danny.

"No, I didn't," says Mr. Mozzarella.
"But why don't you stay and help me
make this valentine?" he asks.
"Not today," says Danny's mother.
She is getting tired. "It's time for us
to go home. See you tomorrow."

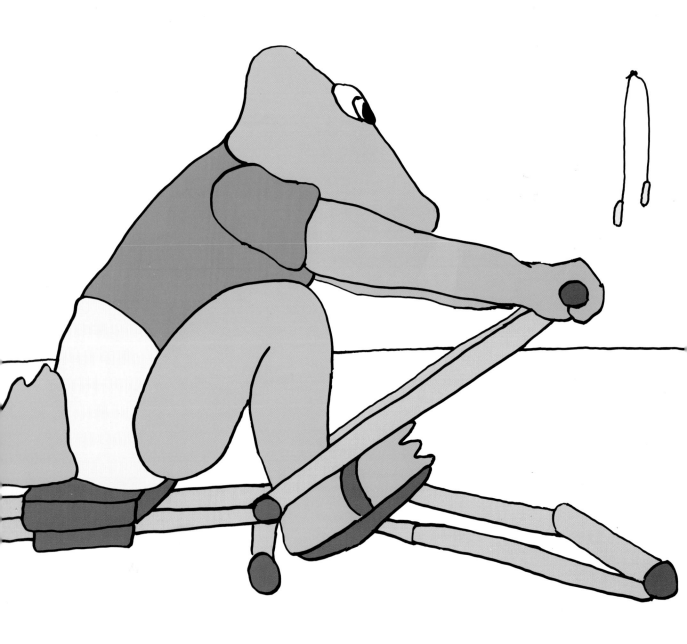

Danny and his mother go home.
There is Danny's father. He is rowing
on his rowing machine.
"Daddy, did you send me this heart?"
asks Danny.

"No, Danny, I didn't. But I know who
did!" says his father.
"Who did? Who did?" cries Danny.
"Open that door and you will see,"
answers Danny's father.

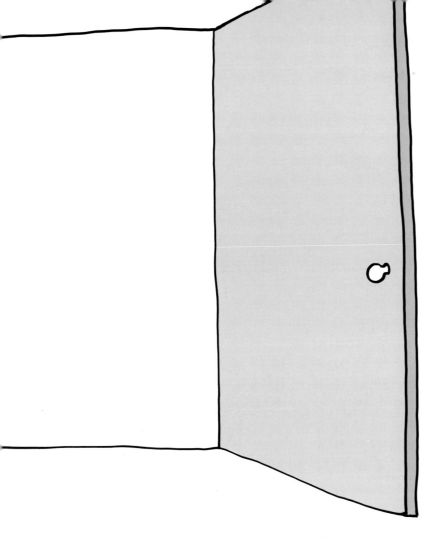

Danny opens the door.
There is Granny!
"I sent the valentine to my favorite
valentine boy," says Granny.
And she gives Danny a great big
Valentine's Day hug.